The Classification

and Coding of

11 762578

Learning Resources
Centre

First published 1986
Revised 1992 by:
The Chartered Institute of Management Accountants

ISBN 0 948036 88 5

Contents

Page

About this series . . ./About this book . . .

Preface/Acknowledgement

1 The Elements of Classification and Coding   1

1.1	General introduction	1
1.2	Classification	1
1.3	Codes	8
1.4	Summary and conclusions	9

2 The Classification Process   11

2.1	Introduction	11
2.2	The process	11
2.3	Summary of the classification process	23

3 Classification in Accounts and Reports   27

3.1	Introduction	27
3.2	The number of classifications	27
3.3	Aggregation	30
3.4	The accounting contribution	37
3.5	Summary and conclusions	41

4 Coding   43

4.1	Introduction	43
4.2	Qualities of good coding	43
4.3	Types of code	45
4.4	Coding errors	50
4.5	Computer developments and coding	54
4.6	Summary and conclusions	55

5 Conclusions   57

References   58

About this series . . .

Developments in Information Technology (IT) have transformed the business environment in recent years and there is every sign that the pace of technological advancement will continue to accelerate in the future. Whilst there are obvious advantages to be gained from the more sophisticated and efficient treatment of information, these developments have also brought many problems, particularly in the way in which traditional organisational structures and disciplines have had to be adapted to accommodate the various changes. The finance function is frequently at the centre of such developments and management accountants, in particular, have been quick to realise the need to keep abreast of evolving technology and to review it suitably for their own information systems.

The Management Information System series has been introduced by the Institute to assist with the task of keeping the management accountant informed as to the current developments in the area of IT and their implications in practical terms. The books will cover diverse subject matters, linked by the IT theme, and will include the 'latest' issues as well as consolidating on more established areas. The books are intended to provide an easy-to-read introduction to the subject areas and, whilst they cannot be exhaustive in content, it is hoped that sufficient material is present in each to provide a sound basis for proceeding to more detailed study or practical application. The editor will welcome suggestions for future publications.

About this book . . .

There are few business applications for which the processes of classification and coding do not play a significant role. In fact in any but the most trivial of applications much of the subsequent success of the system will depend upon the level of attention paid to these aspects during the pre-implementation period. Whilst most accountants will by now be familiar with many of the principles and techniques for coding, for example in the definition of nominal account codes, the concepts of classification may appear to be rather more foreign. It is, however, the process of classification of data which is initially of greater importance in the analysis of information requirements to be derived from a system. It is only after the structure of the information under review has been determined that it becomes possible successfully to define a coding system which will enable processing to generate the required reports and analyses easily.

In this book, first published in 1986 and now appropriately updated, Roland Fox clearly outlines the basic principles underlying the theory of both classification and coding and sets this theory in context of many practical examples drawn from an accounting environment.

Following an introduction to both elements, the reader is guided through the process of classification in three stages, those of: entity analysis, derivation of data requirements and, finally, data classification. There follows a chapter specifically relating to the application of classification to accounting systems, before the subject of coding is tackled in the final chapter.

The reader should be left with a fuller understanding of the nature of data relating, both directly and indirectly, to the accounting process and, just as importantly, be better equipped to define and manage the production of relevant information which is of corporate benefit. This is, after all, one of the principal functions of the modern management accountant and, as the author states, issues in designing reports and accounts can no longer be regarded as relating solely to the accounting function.

Roland Fox is a lecturer in the Department of Business and Management Studies at the University of Salford.

Ray Franks/Series Editor

Acknowledgement

I would like to thank the many firms, both large and small, who gave up their valuable time to take part in the background research for this monograph. I would also like to express my gratitude to Bernard Cox, formerly of CIMA, for his patient guidance, and to Professor Robert Scapens of Manchester University whose advice and encouragement has immeasurably improved the following pages.

1986   *Roland Fox*

Changes in the Second Edition of this monograph have been restricted to a number of small amendments and additions to the original text.

1992   *Roland Fox*

Preface

The previous monograph by the Institute of Cost and Management Accountants on classification and coding was published in 1956. Since that time, there have been far-reaching changes in the subject, which have necessitated this completely revised edition.

The principal cause of change has been the use of computers to process accounting information. The priorities that governed the design of codes in a manual system cannot be directly translated into its computerised counterpart. Due account must be taken of the more sophisticated equipment for inputting codes, as well as the implications of the new methods for sorting and storing data.

The concepts used for classifying data have also been subject to substantial changes. The increased ability of the computer to process information has enabled the accountant to consider a much wider range of information than was previously practicable. New methodologies have been developed that enable the accountant, and more generally, information users to examine their classification requirements and present them in a manner that is compatible with the new systems.

Accompanying this information revolution, as it is sometimes called, has been a change in the responsibilities of the accountant. Whereas previously he would be required to design, operate and develop the largely manual system, these tasks are nowadays specialist functions in their own right, requiring systems analysts, data administrators and programmers. The accountant's role is increasingly that of the 'informed user'. In other words, the accountant is more the customer of the computerised information system rather than the designer; in his new role, he must understand and be able to exploit the abilities of the computer without necessarily having to be familiar with the detailed construction of the system.

The aim of this monograph has been to incorporate the technological changes with the more traditional aspects of the subject to produce a practical guide to effective classification and coding. This approach has necessitated the inclusion of certain fundamental computer-related concepts. Care has been taken to use these concepts only in so far as they affect the accountant's task. Accordingly, the technical aspects of any new term have been avoided, and it is assumed that the reader has no specialist knowledge of computers. However, many of the terms will be found in CIMA's *Computing Terminology* should readers experience any difficulties.

1
The Elements of Classification and Coding

1.1 General introduction

The processes of classification and coding are the first steps to creating order and meaning in an information system. All the information that management receive will be subject to some form of classification, and in order to record, store and retrieve classifications, a code will be required. Effective management will depend upon the way in which data is classified and coded. For example, poor sales of a particular product are not likely to be recognised by management if an organisation only classifies its sales by area. Also, if an unsuitable code is used there may be considerable problems in handling the information however classified. An organisation, therefore, cannot expect to be able to take effective decisions or carry out effective planning and control unless it has reviewed very carefully its data requirements (i.e., classifications) and the way such data is to be recorded (i.e., coded).

The purpose of this monograph is to examine the problems posed by these two concepts in the design of accounting information. In this chapter, the meaning and incidence of classification and coding of accounting information are discussed. Chapter 2 concerns the process of classifying data. Chapter 3 examines the problems of translating classifications into accounts and reports. Chapter 4 looks at the coding of data, and, finally, Chapter 5 summarises the main issues. Unless stated otherwise, it is assumed throughout that information is being processed on a computerised system, though, as mentioned in the preface, no special expertise with computers is assumed.

1.2 Classification

1.2.1 A definition

'Classification' is a term that at first sight might seem to need little explanation. It is a familiar part of most areas of human knowledge, there being a classification of plants in botany, chemicals in chemistry, numbers in mathematics, and so on. It might be argued that accounting classifies financial data in a similar manner; for example, expenditure might be classified by department, sales by area and profit by product. There is in fact an important difference. Unlike the other areas of knowledge mentioned above, accounting does not have a scheme of classification that is universally accepted. Textbooks suggest classifications[1] and countries impose classifications for external accounting reports[2]. In no case, however, has a set of classifications been devised that has had anything more than a limited acceptance for a limited number of purposes. Certainly, accounting cannot offer classifications as significant as those in the aforementioned sciences. Further, in view of the increasing diversity of organisations, it is unlikely that any future attempts to create an all-embracing set of classifications in accounting will be successful.

In practice, therefore, the accountant has to create a classification of information that is suited to the particular organisation that he serves, and even to the particular decisions that management take. For this reason, the accountant has to understand the concept of classification in much greater detail than would at first seem to be necessary. In a modern computerised system, this understanding can only be achieved by employing concepts that have been developed in computer science which describe the way in which information is managed. Accordingly, this guide adopts the following definition of classification[3]:

The process of dividing information into entities, and the subsequent assignment of attributes and their values to each entity so as to permit the unambiguous recording of information.

An entity is an object about which information is stored, this may be tangible, such as a customer, an item of stock or an employee; alternatively the entity may be more abstract, for example, a department, a grouping of products sold or a marketing expense. Each entity represents an object of interest to the managers of the organisation. On its own it does no more than create broad groupings of data. The necessary detail is provided by assigning attributes to each entity. An attribute is a particular aspect or quality of an entity deemed relevant by the firm (see Table 1.1).

In many cases, the choice of attribute is straightforward. For example, in relation to the entity 'sale' the attributes 'date', 'value', 'customer' and 'invoice number' would be required in order to construct a basic financial accounting system. The choice is less obvious when the wider decision-making requirements are considered. In Table 1.1 the attributes 'product' and 'area' have been added to the entity 'sale' as being of possible use for this purpose. There is however no obvious selection; 'delivery cost', 'production cost' and 'elapsed time since order date' might equally well have been added[4].

Table 1.1 Entities and attributes

Entity	Attributes
Sale	Date, Amount, Customer name, Products, Area, Invoice number
Product purchase	Date, Amount, Supplier name, Product, Stock number, Invoice number
Customer	Name, Address, Credit limit, Amount outstanding, Invoices, Payments
Advertising expense	Date, Amount, Supplier, Purpose

The final step in the process of classification is the definition of attribute values for each attribute. Attribute values refer to a series of divisions applied to each attribute in such a way as to ensure that an observation, or item requiring classification, has only one value. So, for instance, the attribute 'date' is usually divided into days. Each sale (the observation) will have only one sale date. Similarly 'amount' is normally divided into pounds sterling and pence, and each sale will have only one value. An example of an unsatisfactory choice of attribute values would be if the attribute 'area' for the entity 'sale' were to be divided into say, North, South, North West, North East, South West and South East of England. A sale in London would be classified as having the attribute value South *and* South East. Clearly, such ambiguity is undesirable and the areas need to be defined so as to be mutually exclusive. In this example there is also the possibility that none of the attribute values are applicable. For example a sale in Scotland, Wales, Northern Ireland or abroad would have none of the attribute values given above. This, too, violates the condition that one value should be applicable to each observation. In order to avoid such a possibility, a 'catch-all' division should be included, in this case 'other areas'. Such 'dustbins' need to be constantly monitored to ensure that the proportion of transactions allocated to them does not insensibly grow. The rules for attribute values do not preclude the possibility that a sale may include products delivered to several areas.

In such a case, each separate area delivery constitutes a separate observation requiring one and only one attribute value.

It is now possible to divide the concept of classification into its constituent elements. Firstly there is the definition of the type of 'object' to be classified (the entity) e.g., a sale, a customer, a department and so on. Secondly, the items of interest in relation to each entity (the attributes) must be listed. Finally, each attribute should be ascribed a range of values (the attribute values). These constituent elements may be used to classify all accounting information processed within the organisation. Figure 1.1 summarises the classification of a sale as described above.

Figure 1.1 Classification of Sales

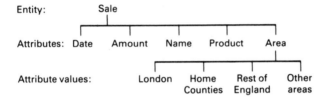

1.2.2 *The occurrence of classification*

The classification of accounting information occurs at three levels of generality or aggregation. These are outlined in Figure 1.2. At the most detailed level is the accounting transaction. This concerns the recording of an event, usually financial in nature, such as the purchase of a product, payment of a debt, sale of a service and so on. The classification of such transactions follows the process outlined in the previous section. Thus a sales transaction may be classified according to Figure 1.1. It is from this information that accounts and reports are constructed, hence its position in Figure 1.2 at the base of the triangle.

The next and most familiar level of classification is the account. Each account consists of a set of transactions whose 'amount' attributes are totalled according to the double-entry convention to produce an account balance. The accountant, when he decides how many different accounts are required to represent expenditure, for instance, is also determining how such expenditure is to be classified. Thus an account entitled 'Department C Labour' will consist of a summation of the amount attribute for all those transactions whose location attribute has the value 'Department C' and whose subject attribute has the value 'Labour'. If these three attributes, amount, location and subject, are not recorded at the transaction level then it will not be possible to construct such an account.

Accounting data is presented to management at the report level. The report consists of a series of classifications of information against which the amount attribute is disclosed. As Figure 1.2 suggests, a classification in a report will usually consist of one or more accounts; hence it is at a more aggregated or summarised level than the account. A report may however, use information recorded at the transaction level only. For instance, using the example of a sale in Figure 1.1, the accountant might open sale accounts based on the attribute area. If a report requires the classification of sales by product, or sales by product and area, then the information will have to be compiled directly from the transaction level. It is only, in this example, if the report requires a classification using area alone that the account may be used.

Finally, although these levels are separately identifiable within any one organisation, there is no such distinction between organisations. Information treated as an account in one system may be the subject of a more detailed report in another. As with the choice of classification, there is a high degree of subjectivity in the design of account and report structures.

Figure 1.2 Levels of classification

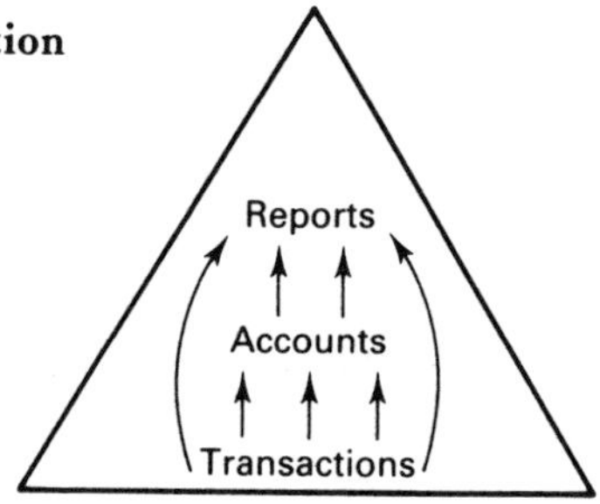

1.2.3 *Value of classification*

It is difficult to measure the precise costs and benefits of any particular scheme of classification of financial data or even to produce a comparative assessment of alternative classifications. As a result, managers are often not fully aware that the scheme chosen to classify data will affect the value of the information presented before them. Behavioural psychologists have noted this phenomenon in observing that 'decision makers tend to use only that information which is explicitly displayed, and only in the form in which it is displayed'[5]. In view of this dependence, it is particularly important that the accountant, as the provider of information, should carefully evaluate the data he produces.

The cost of a scheme of classification will vary greatly depending upon the particular circumstances of the organisation. If there is no existing information system, then computer hardware will have to be purchased along with computer programs, a coding system will have to be devised, and sundry administration costs, such as staff training and the design of input documents, will be incurred. If there is an existing information system, but an inflexible one, many if not all the items required to install a classification scheme may have to be purchased. If however, the organisation operates a sophisticated, flexible information system, a new scheme of classification may be introduced with relative ease. In such a case it is likely that the coding system, computer programs and hardware would need only minor alterations.

In view of this great variability, the cost of a classification scheme cannot in general terms be evaluated. It is not possible therefore to produce a standard cost per classification to be applied in valuing an information system. The most appropriate method to use is relevant costing. This method seeks to establish only those costs that are actually incurred directly as a result of, in this case, a classification decision. The circumstances of each new scheme of classification are considered separately, and any cost apportionment or overhead absorption avoided as far as possible.

The benefits of classification may be defined as the net increase in profits that result from the improved decisions based upon new classifications.* For instance, a new classification of advertising costs may result in improved selling techniques and higher profits; another example would be a revised analysis of labour costs to enable a more effective bonus scheme to be implemented, resulting in lower labour costs per unit and hence higher profits. As with the costs of a scheme of classification, the benefits are not easily quantified, in particular the relationship between improved data and an increase in profits is likely to be highly complex.

---

*non-profit making organisations should substitute the word *efficiency* or *surplus* where the word *profit* is used in this and succeeding sections.

Despite the measurement difficulties, the net benefit of a classification scheme can be very great indeed. The following examples illustrate this point:

- Michael Edwardes on becoming Chairman of British Leyland found that *'there was no breakdown of cost information model by model. The speed with which my colleagues set about making good this mammoth defect was encouraging; imagine trying to run a business without knowing the cost of the individual products – it seemed unbelievable'*[6]. The reorganisation of costs in this manner was a vital element in the subsequent decentralisation of BL on a product basis.

The next two cases concern firms that took part in the background research for this guide.

- An international company owned a small Irish subsidiary that engaged in light engineering on its own account, as well as retailing a limited range of products from companies associated with its parent. The subsidiary was treated as an autonomous unit, and was required to produce only summary figures of its performance which consisted of a single sales figure, costs analysed by subject (i.e., materials, labour, etc.) and a single profit figure. The data had for some years been compared with averages for the group as a whole and was judged to be satisfactory.

This favourable view of the subsidiary's performance altered dramatically when an analysis of sales was carried out by an accountant from the parent company. The purpose of the analysis was to provide details for a local census of production. Retail products were found to comprise 50 per cent of sales. As there were few local costs for such products, the profit from the retailing activity could easily be established. It was found to be greatly in excess of overall profits, implying that the main activity of the firm, light engineering, was running at a considerable loss. As a result of this reclassification of sales the factory was closed down and the retail operations were run from smaller premises.

- A subsidiary of a Dutch firm grew large enough to begin manufacturing at a greenfield site in the North West of England. After several changes of accountant, the local director appointed a finance officer from a large manufacturing firm. Shortly after his appointment, the finance officer greatly increased the number of accounts used to summarise transactions. As an example, where the old system had a single protective clothing account, he opened separate accounts for hats, boots, goggles, etc. The new accountant had, in fact, directly transferred the classifications used by his previous employer, the large manufacturer, to this relatively small firm thereby creating considerable unnecessary complications. This action resulted in extensive errors in coding and misclassification data. Eventually the firm was unable to report even very basic financial information.

From these examples it is clear that classification can have a very great impact on the fortunes of an organisation, and that its importance should not be underestimated merely because there are difficulties in measuring its precise value.

1.3 Codes

1.3.1 Definition

A code is a collection of symbols used to carry information within the system. The process of coding is the translation of information into symbolic form in such a way as to allow the system to store, manipulate and retrieve data in an efficient manner.

There is a close link between classification and coding. As outlined in Section 1.2.1, classification imposes a structure on information, ordering it into entities, attributes and attribute values. It is this structure that determines the contents of the code. The code for an advertising transaction, for instance, will depend upon the attributes that a firm wishes to record. Table 1.1 suggests that the 'supplier' and 'purpose of expenditure' are suitable attributes to code. In this case, each supplier will need his own separate code and the codes for 'purpose' will depend upon the chosen values of that attribute. If 'purpose' is divided according to product, e.g., 'advertising on product C', then the code must be of a suitable format to reflect the number of different products sold. Having coded data in this manner it will then be possible to produce accounts based upon these attributes, e.g., 'advertising in newspaper A' (the supplier attribute) or 'advertising for product A' (the purpose attribute). Further reports may be constructed from such codes, e.g., 'advertising by product and newspaper'.

In order to stress the link with classification as defined in Section 1.2.1, the definition of coding used in this guide is as follows:

An ordered collection of symbols designed to provide a unique identification of the item being encoded as well as identifying the values of attributes chosen by the user.

CIMA similarly stress the link with classification, and defines a code as 'a system of symbols designed to be applied to a classified set of items'[7].

1.3.2 Application of codes

All information used by the accounting department that is in some manner stored or processed by the system will require coding. The account is the most common item that requires a coding structure; however, codes may also be needed to record information concerning customers e.g. different addresses for invoicing and delivery, discount, etc., suppliers, materials, components, finished goods, sales, capital expenditure, plant, employees and any other subject deemed relevant by the organisation. There is no single optimum structure, as the precise format will depend upon the particular needs of the system. It is not surprising, therefore, that codes appear in nearly as many forms as there are organisations.

1.4 Summary and conclusions

This chapter has outlined and discussed the definition of coding and classification in the modern accounting system. In addition, the following conclusions have been drawn:

(1) Classification and coding is fundamental to the design of an information system.

(2) There is no single optimum classification chart or coding scheme applicable to all organisations.

(3) Many issues require managerial judgement.

(4) The importance of computers in information systems has necessitated the inclusion of certain basic computer derived terms in order to be able to understand and exploit their contribution.

The Classification Process

2.1 Introduction

Developments in information technology have greatly enlarged the number of data classifications that the standard information system can manage. As a result, the accountant has a much wider range of information that he can store than under the traditional pre-computerised systems. In order to exploit these developments fully, it is important that the accountant, and the organisation as a whole in which he works, extends its information requirements so as to lead to improved management and thereby improved performance.

The purpose of this chapter is to outline a method that will enable the organisation critically to review and improve its existing classification system. There are, of course, many possible approaches to achieving this aim. In practice, however, certain concepts and methods have been found to be particularly useful with regard to computerised information systems. These methods have, for the most part, originated in the field of study known as systems analysis[8]. In this chapter, these techniques have been combined with the additional concerns of the accountant. The process is described in three stages:

(1) Entity analysis (Section 2.2.2).
(2) Deriving data requirements (Section 2.2.3).
(3) Data classifications (Section 2.2.4).

Together these stages represent a successively detailed analysis of information needs, starting with the whole organisation, and ending with a detailed list of data classifications – their purpose and their links with other data.

2.2 The process

2.2.1 An overview

The previous chapter demonstrated that classifications of data are the substance of accounting reports. In turn, reports form the basis of the accounting information system. Finally, the information system serves to further the goals of the organisation. The process is indivisible. Consequently, a review of data classifications can only sensibly be undertaken by reviewing the goals of the organisation and how the organisation intends to meet the goals *before* assessing the adequacy of the data classifications. For example, many firms place a high priority on maximising the year end published profit and loss account. The classifications of this account, sales, cost of sales, and expenses and profits, therefore play an important part in many reporting systems. Another example would be if a firm considered market share or quality to be important. A good reporting system should measure the attainment of these goals; data relating to quality and market share should be collected and reported.

The overall aim of a classification review, therefore, is to ensure that data classifications meet the goals of the organisation. Despite the evident importance of this exercise it is perhaps surprising to learn that firms rarely, if ever, carry out such an exercise. Even when there is an ideal opportunity to institute such a review, as when there is a takeover or a computer system is being updated, the most common response is to translate the existing classifications directly to the new system.

Three reasons are suggested here for this shortcoming. First, accountants and their fellow managers and directors do not identify the adequacy of the data presented to them as being a part of their managerial brief. As was observed in Section 1.2.3, this is no more than a human failing – managers, in their concern to understand accounting reports and their implications, fail to assess the medium by which the data is transmitted; i.e. the report itself.

Secondly, those closely associated with the system, notably systems analysts and programmers, employ techniques that are descriptive rather than critical, though there is now an increasing realisation that a more evaluative approach is required (see Section 2.2.2).

Thirdly, such reviews are often regarded as unnecessary. Such a view is without justification. Anecdotal evidence has already been offered as to the importance of data classifications (Section 1.2.3). However, the need for fundamental reviews has, especially in recent years, received wide recognition in the literature. For example *Johnson* and *Kaplan*[9] observe:

'Today's management accounting information, driven by the procedures and cycle of the organisation's financial reporting system, is too late, too aggregated

and too distorted to be relevant for managers' planning and control decisions. With increased emphasis on meeting quarterly or annual earnings targets, internal accounting systems focus narrowly on producing a monthly earnings report'.

Alternative approaches that report quality[10], activity [11], and the attainment of strategic goals[12] have been suggested as providing new insights and new bases for reporting the processes of the organisation. The inadequacy of the simple profit and loss account model is now widely recognised. It is not sufficient to report divisions, departments etc. solely as 'bits' of a profit and loss account. Yet this is all too often the essence of many existing systems which remain unreviewed year after year.

Notwithstanding the current state of affairs in many organisations reviews should be:

(1) Regular.

(2) Carried out by senior management.

(3) Given high priority.

The scope of each review should also be as wide as possible, for modern computer systems increasingly take an overall, subject-based rather than a detailed, applications-based view of data. In practical terms, an applications view means that accounting data is stored and retrieved specifically to meet particular accounting applications. If the data is required for other applications by accountants or non-accountants then it is likely that either extensive reprogramming would be required or new files of similar data would have to be created. Such an approach is both expensive and wastes scarce resources. The alternative subject-based approach considers all the accounting and non-accounting applications of a set of data. This enables the data to be stored in a manner that is flexible or independent of any one application[13], making it more useful to the organisation.

A second reason for having a wide-ranging review is that the decisions that classifications are designed to support are not necessarily limited to any one of the traditional subject areas, for example, selling decisions involve marketing and accounting information, while stocking decisions involve marketing, accounting and production information. The inclusion of all the relevant data will enable management to consider interdependencies between subject areas and thus greatly enhance the quality of information.

Such reviews are team exercises requiring input from all management. External management consultants and computer consultants may also be required to enhance professional expertise for such an exercise. In general, it must be recognised that the business of managing data is central to the success of any organisation.

2.2.2 *Entity analysis*

The exercise begins with entity analysis. This technique serves as a means of creating general groupings of data, prior to more detailed analysis. Although originally intended to be a descriptive technique, it has since been adapted to become the basis of a critical review of the information system. To illustrate this point, *Martin*[14] quotes an entity analysis consultant as follows:

A number of different types of company had been taken over, over the years . . . each wanted its own systems. Each has got its own ordering system, different types of purchase order numbers, different stock numbers . . . The entity analysis method is a way for the user management to see the types of problems they are inflicting upon themselves by not rationalising the system.

The term 'entity' has the same meaning as in Section 1.2.1 and refers to an object, real or abstract, about which information is stored. Unfortunately, there is no standard methodology for entity analysis, each version differing slightly[15]. This study is no exception. Here, a method is outlined using concepts and structures familiar to the accounting function.

An unambiguous starting point for this process is the administrative structure of the organisation. A firm, for example, that is divisionalised on the basis of products, can reasonably be expected to group much of its information according to the chosen product classification. Alternatively, if the firm is separated according to area, then the areas concerned would serve as the basis for reporting much of its information. In general, a division or similar administrative unit will represent a major grouping of information within the organisation.

Usually such administrative units will be too general to serve as the basis for further analysis. Therefore, still using the organisation structure as a guide, each division can be further broken down into departments and sections or their equivalents (see Figure 2.1). Each section should consist of a set of closely related tasks that cannot usefully be subdivided without breaking such ties. For example, it might be considered that the management accounting section should be separated into costing, reporting and budgeting subsections. In most organisations, though, these subsections will make use of the same data and will need to work closely together, making such a division of limited value for data management purposes.

Figure 2.1 Determining manageable entities

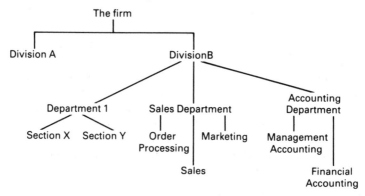

Another means of determining useful grouping of data is to examine staff responsibilities. Closely related tasks and data will tend to be grouped together and assigned to one manager. In most cases, there will be a close affinity between staff responsibilities and administrative structure. Where there are differences, a review will be required to establish the most appropriate grouping of data.

In this manner, the information requirements of the firm can be divided into a series of sections grouped by department and division. A section, however, does not of itself indicate what information is required. It is the activities carried out within the section that are the source of the demand for data. Accordingly entity analysis is completed by considering the activities carried out by the entity.

In practice it has been found that a well defined activity should have the following properties[16]:

(1) There should be a clearly identifiable outcome, i.e., a decision, report or action.
(2) The boundaries of the activity should be clearly defined. It should therefore be possible to determine unambiguously where the activity is being carried out.

(3) There should be a clear understanding by management as a whole on who is responsible for the activity and who should carry it out.
(4) An activity is likely to be linked to other activities within the same entity and activities in other entities. Such linkages should be kept to a minimum.

Using this guide to outlining activities, stage one of the overall strategy is completed by mapping or relating entities to activities in the manner of Table 2.1.

More recently the concept of activity based costing has become very popular, particularly in the United States. However, the origins of the use of the term activity in this text is rooted in systems analysis and not in this more recent development. To distinguish between the two, activity based costing is generally represented as identifying the variable nature of fixed costs and relating these costs ultimately to production. Here, the use of the term 'activity' is more general, serving only as as basis for determining related data of whatever nature and for whatever purpose.

2.2.3 *Deriving data requirements*

The purpose of stage two of the analysis is to develop a methodology for creating relevant data for each activity. In some cases, the relevant data is obvious. For example, the completion of a tax return, or the preparation of the Annual Report, are activities that specify clearly what information is required. By contrast, in much of the internal decision-making activities there will be a certain amount of choice as to what data is required. From Table 2.1, activities such as manpower planning, predicting future profits and analysing promotion expenses can be carried out from widely differing sets of data. The problem of making this choice and selecting information to present to management is one that is familiar to accountants everywhere. This stage is therefore a generalised summary of the methodological approach advocated in many of the more recent accounting and accounting related texts.[17]

Firstly, there is the need to have objectives; without some understanding of the purpose of a particular managerial activity, a review would not be possible. Secondly, a model needs to be constructed 'expressing relationships between fundamental variables and values reflected in the objectives'[18]. For example, if the objective is to increase profits by 20 per cent, the appropriate model would examine those variables such as sales price, production quantity, stock levels and costs that affect profits. Relationships between variables may be expressed using mathematical methods, words and/or diagrams. Once constructed, the model enables management to examine the effect of differing decisions and events on the firm's objectives.

Table 2.1 An example of activity analysis from the data grouping of Figure 2.1

Department	Activity
Personnel	Recruiting
	Negotiating rates
	Monitoring headcounts
	Helping with disputes
	Eductation & training
	Public relations
	Manpower planning
	Recording employee history
	Authorising deduction
	Administering pensions
Accounting	*Finance*
	Creditor management
	Debtor management
	Cash flow planning
	Compiling year end accounts
	Capital investment planning
	Management
	Costing
	Budget planning
	Monitoring present performance
	Predicting future profits
	Investigating deviations from plans
	Controlling stock levels
	Salesmen's bonus calculation
Sales	*Order processing:*
	Monitoring of orders
	Helping with manufacturing schedules
	Checking invoices against orders
	Chasing late orders
	Sales
	Allocating sales targets
	Sales predictions
	Debt collection
	Analysing salesmen's expenses
	Assessing effectiveness of expenditure
	Assessing new products
	Improving customer relations

Finally, a model requires information. The variables used in the model will indicate the type of information classification that is required. Thus, for example, a product-pricing model may require as input the amount spent on labour, materials and advertising by product, which is in effect a classification of costs by subject and purpose (see Section 3.4.2). The relationship between the objectives, model and data requirements of an activity is expressed in Figure 2.2, and an example is given in Figure 2.3.

Figure 2.2 The process of determining data requirements

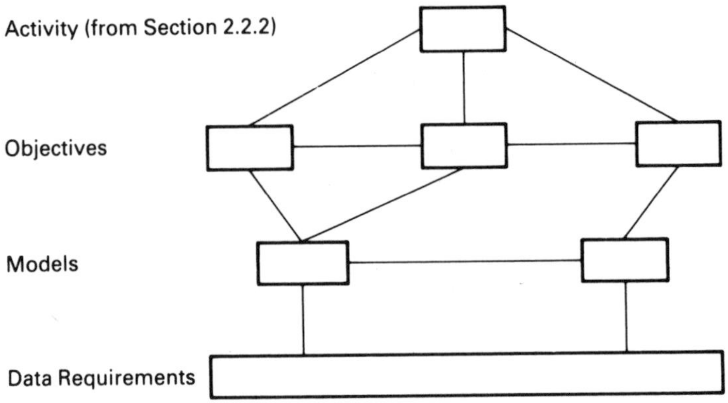

In practice each of the stages in Figure 2.2 present considerable practical problems. These are now considered in turn.

(a) Objectives

Ideally, an objective should be the clearly identifiable result of a well defined activity. In practice, such clarity can often only be obtained by specifying several goals, rather than a single goal. For example, the stock-control activity outlined in Figure 2.3 could have been attributed with the single objective of the 'efficient management of stock'. Such a goal lacks sufficient clarity to serve as the basis of any model. It is therefore necessary to have a series of more specific operational goals that indicate more clearly the appropriate models that are required.

Having more than one goal for an activity does not imply that they are in harmony with each other. On the contrary, a certain amount of conflict is likely to be the norm. For example, in Figure 2.3, the goal of minimising stock-management costs on its own will require minimal stock levels; this action conflicts with the need to avoid stock outs by holding a buffer stock. Such problems are a natural part of the decision-making process, as *Cyert* and *March*[19] observe:

Since the existence of unresolved conflict is a conspicuous feature of organisations, it is exceedingly difficult to construct a useful positive theory of organisational decision-making if we insist on internal goal consistency.

Figure 2.3 An application of the data requirements model of Figure 2.2

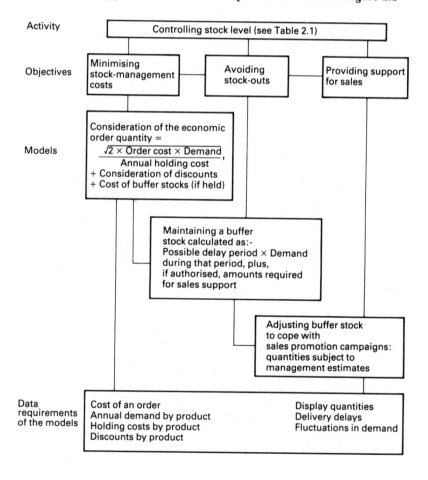

(b) The model

A model may reflect one or more of the objectives of an activity. Just as the objectives are linked, so there is a link between the models. A cash-flow planning model, for instance, will require input from sales and purchasing models. Models may also conflict as a consequence of the goal conflict discussed above. Goal and model conflict may be avoided by establishing trade-offs; for example, in Figure 2.3 the need to avoid stock-outs may be made compatible with the need to minimise stock-management costs, by requiring all relevant models to provide for one month's demand in the buffer stock, thus reducing any dispute over the actual level.

Devising a model is not an easy process. There are, fortunately, several useful methods, including statistical model building, simulation methods, heuristic approaches and the descriptive/ analytical procedures of systems analysis[20]. These methods are suitable for the strategy described here providing that they express in an unambiguous manner their data requirements. In general, simple models are preferred because they have clearer data requirements. However, even very complex models may yet be clear in this respect, in that the main difficulties often arise from the interaction of the variables in such models rather than the variables themselves[21], hence their data requirements may nevertheless be unambiguous.

In devising models to describe management activity, there is a danger that the exercise may be seen as setting a standard procedure for decision taking. This would be undesirable. Management styles change, objectives change and the activities themselves change over time. Likewise, the models should also change to reflect these developments. It is important therefore that the need for flexibility and change is recognised; periodic reviews of the extent to which the models remain appropriate are needed.

(c) Data requirements

The product of stage two of this strategy is a statement of the data requirements of the organisation as in Figure 2.3 and Table 2.2.

Difficulties in specifying data requirements should be judged in terms of the model that they are intended to serve. Thus, for example, the specification of holding costs in Figure 2.3 can be defined from the Economic Order Quantity (EOQ) model, as excluding allocated fixed costs and including the cost of working capital tied up in stock. This definition follows directly from the EOQ model itself.

Table 2.2 Individual data requirements

For controlling retail stock levels	Cost of an order
	Estimated annual demand by product, using orders and sales patterns
	Holding costs by product
	Discount by product
	Display quantities,
	Delivery delays by product
	Fluctuations in demand
For predicting profits	Orders by product, division, time, £'s, units
	Sales by product, division, time, £'s, units
	Variable costs by product
	Fixed costs by time

2.2.4 Data classification

The data requirements specified in Section 2.2.3 form the basis of the formal classification of data in a manner suitable for translating into a computerised information system. This is achieved by applying the concepts of entities, attributes and attribute values, as outlined in Section 1.2.1.

The first task is to group the data into entities. In Section 2.2.2, data requirements were formed into broad organisational based entities, comprising departments, sections and so on. For this stage of the analysis, more detailed entities are required that represent groupings of attributes required by the data models. By comparing the requirements of the various models, unnecessary duplication can be eliminated. For instance, the activities of 'controlling stock levels' and 'profit predictions' (see Figure 2.1) are both likely to be supported by models requiring details concerning orders and sales. These details may be expressed by one entity for orders and one entity for sales, each entity would then serve both models. In Table 2.2 the data requirements of the 'controlling stock level' activity, developed in Figure 2.3, are listed with the suggested data required for 'sales predictions' (the model for deriving profit prediction data has been omitted). This list of data requirements is then joined up in Table 2.3 to produce a subject-based classification chart, where the attributes of one entity serve many activities.

As the data requirements increase with the consideration of more and more activities, so entities and attributes may be redesigned. In Table 2.3 for instance, it is likely that the orders by month and sales by month that have been identified as attributes of the entity 'product', would, with the consideration of more activities, become attributes of other entities such as the 'budget' as in Table 2.3. It may be preferable, ultimately, to have orders and sales as separate entities. As the picture is completed relationships will appear as in Figure 2.4, activities will tend to cluster the entities into entity supergroups that can then be used as the basis for subsequent formation of databases.

Table 2.3 Combined requirements

Activity	Entity	Attributes
	Product	Product name, standard costs, division, orders by month, sales by month, supplier, holding costs, order cost
Profit prediction	Supplier	Name, price, product discounts, delivery time, recorded delays
	Budget	Orders, sales, stock level, month, product
	Variable costs	Product, amount
	Fixed cost	Time, amount
Stock control	Display	Product, quantity, time

The process of outlining data classifications is completed by listing the values associated with each attribute. In some cases the values will be self evident, e.g., sales should be in monetary units, and quantities, a supplier's name as an attribute should have values such as a number that identifies each supplier. In other cases, careful reference to the appropriate decision models is required; for example, sales classified by area require consideration as to what areas are most appropriate for sales planning, marketing, administration and so on.

Before a data classification chart in the form of Figure 2.4 can be used as the basis of a computerised information system, there are many technical issues, involving updating, deletion and development of data, as well as computer hardware and software limitations, to be considered. Such matters are the concern of the systems analyst and computer specialist who may require substantial redrawing of the type of chart in Figure 2.4. In such a case, it is the accountant's role to ensure that, as far as is economically possible, the use to which data will be put, as determined by Sections 2.2.2 and 2.2.3 of this strategy, will not be obstructed by computer and systems-related problems.

Figure 2.4 Entities and clusters

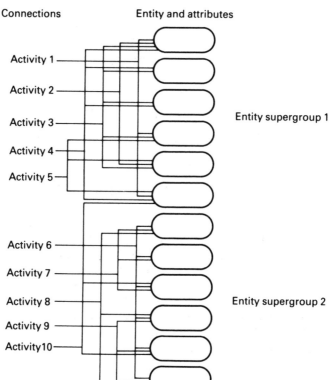

2.3 Summary of the classification process

Classifications of data cannot be devised independently of the organisation that they are intended to serve. Accordingly, Section 2.2 has described a detailed approach to assessing appropriate data classification that is based on an analysis of the organisation. In stage one of the analysis (Section 2.2.2) the organisation was described in terms of units undertaking relatively independent activities. In the second stage (Section 2.2.3), each activity was modelled using a combination of managerial experience and the accountant's specialist knowledge of the use of information for decision-making, planning and control. The model provides the source of the data requirements of the organisation, which in the final stage of the analysis (Section

Figure 2.5 General Classification Model

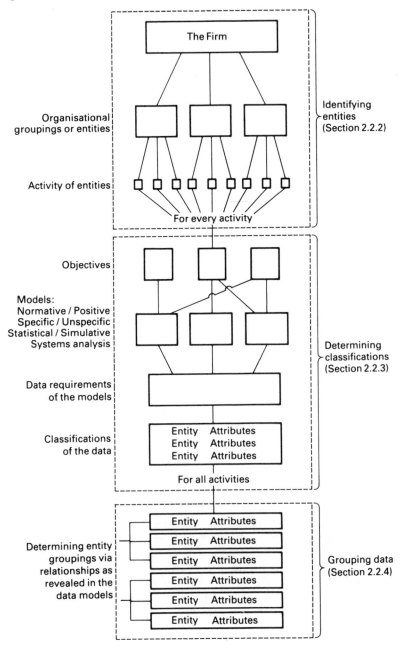

2.2.4) is translated into the formal classification structure consisting of entities, attributes and attribute values as described in Tables 2.2 and 2.3 and Figure 2.4. The overall strategy is summarised in Figure 2.5.

In order to translate the classification requirements into a computerised system, much further specialised analysis will be undertaken by systems analysts, programmers and other information specialists. By deriving and presenting classifications in the manner described above, such specialists receive an unambiguous picture of user requirements. The accountant, in turn, should be able to communicate more effectively with other members of the data management team, by using basic terms and concepts in computer science.

3
Classification in Accounts and Reports

3.1 Introduction

The previous chapter outlined a methodology for producing classifications of information that is applicable to both accounting and non-accounting functions within the organisation. In applying the methodology to an accounting system, there will be special problems associated with each of the many forms of accounting output.

This chapter concentrates on the two principal areas of accounting classification; namely, the chart of account and the accounting report. The following issues are examined:

(1) The need to limit the number of classifications.
(2) The effect of aggregating transactions into accounts and reports.
(3) Accounting conventions in designing and presenting classifications.

A chart of accounts is simply a listing of all the accounts used by the firm. The account, as discussed in Section 1.2.2, is a classification of financial transactions. Thus the account entitled 'department A labour' is a classification of expenditure transactions using the attributes 'department' and 'type of expenditure'; a debtor account is a classification of unpaid revenues by customer and so on. An accounting report is the presentation of information for managerial purposes. Often the report may simply reproduce a particular selection of accounts. In most cases, however, there will also be a summing up or aggregation of accounts in certain areas, as well as the use of information or attributes derived directly from classifications made at the transaction level.

3.2 The number of classifications

The number of classifications possible in an accounting system will depend upon the number of entities, attributes, and attribute values chosen to describe the financial transaction. The potential number is much greater than would appear from a listing in the manner of Table 2.3. For example, supposing a firm chose to record the attributes of the entity sales as in Table 3.1. If every classification included the date and total amount due, then there would be five remaining attributes for classifying data.

Table 3.1 Attributes of the entity 'Sale'

Entity	Attributes
Sale	Date/Amount/Products/Customer/Salesman/Area/Method of Collection/

These attributes alone and in combination are capable of specifying 31 *types* of classification; examples include sales classified by customer, by product, by salesman, by area and by method of collection, as well as combinations, such as sales classified by customer and product or by customer, product and salesman. The number of *actual* classifications will also depend upon the number of attribute values. If in Table 3.1 there were ten customers, ten products, ten salesmen, ten areas and ten methods of collection then there would by no fewer than 161,050 possible classifications; examples include sales to customer A, sales of product one, sales of product one to customer A, sales of product two to customer A, and so on.

Clearly, although an information system may be capable of recording the entities and attributes deemed relevant by the accountant, it will not be able to report all possible classifications. The necessary selection will depend upon the requirements that result from the strategy described in the previous chapter and the limitations in the capacity of the reporting system. It is this latter quality that is of particular importance in accounts and reports.

Capacity constraints occur in the following areas:

(1) Storage files.
(2) Coding capacity.
(3) The accounting report.
(4) Management time.

The constraints imposed by the first two items can be established fairly easily. Overloaded computer files will have high information-retrieval times, and will eventually reject data. The process of coding data is also restricted, in that most forms of code and all accounting systems are limited in the number of items that can be recorded. Also, the ability of the organisation to record data will be restricted by the number of coding clerks, data-entry points, and other physical aspects of the process. If the organisation lacks the capacity to make and record its classifications, then there will be an excessive number of coding errors, delays in preparing data, and misleading reports.

The limitations of the accounting report and management time, are far more difficult to establish. An accounting report is limited by the amount of time available for its preparation and subsequent analysis. The manager receiving a report will tend to limit the effort devoted to its analysis. The time required is variable, and a manager and accounting department may reschedule their work in order to devote more time to important or complex reports. However, the point at which this becomes impossible is largely a matter of managerial judgement and is difficult to measure objectively.

In general, where capacity is exceeded, the organisation must choose between investing in a larger information system or attenuating the classifications to be processed. If it is decided to limit the number of classifications, then their use in accounts and reports must be critically reviewed.

The main elements in such a review are the decision models that the information is designed to serve. If the information requirements of a model create capacity limitations, then it will be necessary to assess the contribution made by each of the variables hitherto included in the model. A useful framework for such an assessment is provided by the law of requisite variety.

The concept of requisite variety seeks to explain how a goal-directed system is able to achieve desired results consistently in differing environments. This is, of course, very much the problem of an organisation striving to achieve its objectives. The law states that the number of controls must be sufficient to reflect the variety of possible states of the system, if undesirable outcomes are to be avoided[22]. In this context control is provided by classification of data.

The example of the Irish factory in Section 1.2.3 provides a useful illustration of the potential use of this method in devising reports.

The factory concerned reported monthly profit and loss figures to the parent company principally to aid the decision as to whether there were matters requiring senior management attention. The classifications deemed important consisted of a summarised traditional profit and loss account that did not distinguish between production and resale. The problem was that the classifications in the profit and loss account failed to reflect the significant environments facing the firm as outlined in Table 3.2. A separate classification of production and resale profits was required. In this case an increase in the variety of classifications in the report was required to ensure adequate control. Equally, in the case of the Dutch firm in Section 1.2.3, a consideration of the significant environments faced by the firm would have shown that there were too many classifications being reported, in that many of the categories were not helping the firm to achieve its goals.

Table 3.2 Requisite Variety of Irish factory example

Environment		Requisite variety
I	Successful Production Successful Resale	YES
II	Unsuccessful Production Successful Resale	NO
III	Successful Production Unsuccessful Resale	NO
IV	Unsuccessful Production Unsuccessful Resale	YES

YES = requisite variety, i.e., sufficient classifications to detect this state

NO = insufficient variety, i.e., insufficient classifications to detect this state

The methodology for applying the concept of requisite variety may be outlined as follows:

(1) Define the goals.
(2) Specify the decision models designed to meet the selected goals.
(3) Detail the environments within which each decision model is expected to achieve its respective goals.
(4) List the classifications required by the model to meet the desired goals in each environment.

In general, a firm must seek to establish the limit to the number of classifications that can be reported if the problem of overcapacity is to be avoided. The concept of requisite variety provides a means of reviewing capacity by examining how each classification contributes to the ability of the organisation to achieve its goals in various environments.

3.3 Aggregation

Classifications in accounts and reports are formed by adding together or aggregating accounting transactions. The principal effect of aggregating data is to lose information at a detailed level in order to create useful data at a more strategic level. A classification of expenses into total cost, for instance, conceals details concerning individual expenses; similarly, a classification of sales into product categories conceals the sales of the individual products, yet both aggregations may be required to present an overall view of profitability. As all possible classifications cannot be presented because the capacity of the system is limited, the organisation must make choices involving the aggregation of data.

This section develops a measure of aggregation derived from information theory, which can be applied to accounting data.

3.3.1 Relative entropy

Relative entropy is a measure of the degree to which totals in accounting are divided into greater detail. It is the inverse of aggregation. This division is most apparent in report structures where totals are subdivided into smaller classifications. A labour report, for instance, will divide total labour costs into smaller classifications, such as labour costs by product, by department or by both, or by other attributes. In the classifications chosen for the labour report, some classes may be highly aggregated encompassing most of the transactions, whereas others may have a very low aggregation comprising only one or two transactions.

The degree of disaggregation or relative entropy is measured as:

Actual disaggregation (or entropy) divided by the total possible disaggregation (or entropy) for the given number of classifications available

Actual entropy is measured by the formula[23]:

$$\text{Entropy } (e) = \sum_{i=1}^{n} \text{pi } \log_2 1/\text{pi}$$

where pi is the class value/total value, n is the total number of classes and $\log_2$ is the logarithm to the base 2.

Table 3.3 illustrates how this formula is applied to a simple report where the total of £3.4m is divided into two classes. The lower the percentage of a class with respect to the total, the higher the degree of disaggregation (this assumes that the transactions are of a similar size).

The element of the formula reflecting this measure is $\log_2 1/pi$. In Table 3.3, Class 1 is far more disaggregated than Class 2, with individual entropy measures of 5.06 and 0.04, respectively. The overall entropy of 0.19 is simply a weighted average of the individual entropies.

Table 3.3 Entropy calculation

	Report £000	%	Entropy calculation pi	1/pi	$\log_2 1/pi$	$pi \times \log_2 1/pi$
Class 1	100	3	0.03	33.33	5.06	0.15
Class 2	3300	97	0.97	1.03	0.04	0.04
Total	3400	100	1.00			
					Entropy =	0.19

This measure indicates two ways of reducing the level of aggregation. Firstly the report may be extended. From the example in Table 3.3, the main area of aggregation is in Class 2 with an individual entropy measure of 0.04. If this class were to be divided into 33 classes of £100 each, then they would all have the entropy measure of Class 1, i.e., 5.06. Secondly, a report may divide a total figure more equally among the available classes. Maximum entropy is achieved where a total is divided equally amongst its constituent classes, as is illustrated in Table 3.4. In such a case $pi = 1/n$ and the maximum entropy can therefore be measured as $E = \log_2 n$. Given this, the formula for relative entropy can now be expressed as:

$$\frac{\text{Actual entropy}}{\text{Maximum entropy}} = \frac{\displaystyle\sum_{i=1}^{n} pi \log_2 1/pi}{\log_2 n} \times 100$$

Table 3.4 A report with maximum entropy

Item	Report £000	%	Entropy calculation pi	1/pi	$\log_2 1/pi$	$pi \times \log_2 1/pi$
Class 1	850	25	0.25	4	2	0.5
Class 2	850	25	0.25	4	2	0.5
Class 3	850	25	0.25	4	2	0.5
Class 4	850	25	0.25	4	2	0.5
	3400					
					Actual entropy	= 2.00
					Maximum entropy $\log_2 4$	= 2.00

Relative entropy has a 0 per cent to 100 per cent scale, where 100 per cent represents the maximum disaggregation given the number of available classes. The measure may also be applied to individual classes in the form:

$$\frac{\log_2 1/p_i}{\log_2 n} \times 100$$

Here, 100 per cent indicates the size of class that, if reported by every other class, would lead to maximum relative entropy. Other values should be seen in relation to this ideal size; thus a larger classification will indicate that not enough detail is being disclosed, giving rise to an individual entropy figure below 100 per cent, a smaller figure will have an entropy figure above 100 per cent, indicating that the figure is too detailed for one class, forcing others to be too large (see Table 3.5).

3.3.2 Application of the measure

Relative entropy serves as a useful critique of the effect of aggregation. To illustrate this point, in Table 3.3 the measure is applied to a report taken from *Horngren's* management accounting textbook[24]. Here the measure clearly shows a great imbalance between the classes. The total entropy of 51 per cent is a low figure, reflecting the fact that the first two classes contain 91 per cent of the total cost. This is also revealed in detail by the high and low individual relative entropy measures. A more disaggregated report would be achieved if the larger classifications were to be divided up into smaller classes. For example, direct materials and labour might usefully be split into direct labour product A, direct materials product A, direct labour product B, direct materials product B and so on. If the report can be extended then such further classifications can simply be added on. If, however, the report is of fixed length owing to capacity considerations, then the relative entropy can be increased by substituting further divisions of labour and materials for the smaller divisions of rework, supplies and small tools, in order to achieve an effect similar to that illustrated in Table 3.4. Examples such as this are not uncommon. One firm visited during the background research reported in the same monthly management report one account of over £1m followed by other accounts of less than £100.

It is important to emphasise that the measure is best used as a critique, indicating areas of exceptionally high and low aggregation. It would be misleading to use the measure as a sole criterion. In Table

3.5, for instance, there may be good reason for reporting that particular set of classifications. The advantage of using the measure of relative entropy is that it creates an awareness that each classification occupies valuable managerial time, and should not be the subject of irrelevant detail or over generalised classifications.

Table 3.5 Application of entropy measure

Item	$000	% of total cost	pi × log2l/pi	Relative entropy of each class %
Direct materials	140.0	59.3	0.45	27
Direct labour	75.0	31.8	0.53	59
Set-up	12.0	5.1	0.22	154
Rework	6.0	2.5	0.13	189
Supplies	0.6	0.3	0.02	307
Small tools	0.9	0.4	0.03	286
Other costs	1.5	0.6	0.05	259
Total controllable costs	236.0	100.0	1.43	

$$\text{Overall relative entropy} = \frac{1.43}{\log_2 7} = 51\%$$

3.3.3 Aggregation and uncertainty

Much accounting data is concerned with estimates of future costs and revenues. Budgets, capital investment plans, quotes, pricing decisions, choice of supplier and so on all require estimates of accounting data. Typically, such estimates are built up from more familiar components. The budget profits for the coming year will, for instance, be built up from budget costs and revenues of the individual products or services. Alternatively, a capital investment plan will involve the combination of resources, the cost of some may be familiar, others less so. In each case important totals such as budget profit or a contract quote will be derived by adding or aggregating cost and revenue estimates. An important question that arises is: if we know the uncertainty of the individual costs and revenues, what will be the uncertainty of their total? Uncertainty may be due to many factors; output levels, inflation, market conditions, exchange rate fluctuations, the decision maker's lack of knowledge and so on. All these uncertainties may be expressed in the form of subjective probabilities of possible outcomes[25]. Uncertainty can then be expressed as the spread of possible returns – a suitable measure of spread often used in finance is the standard deviation. To calculate the standard deviation it is assumed that the decision maker can, for any individual classification, estimate a range of costs or revenues and their associated probability thus:

Scenarios (i)	A Possible cost of repairs (£'s)	B Subjective probability
1	8000	0.25
2	10000	0.50
3	14000	0.25

Expected value　　(E)　$= \Sigma (A_i \times B_i) = 10500$

Standard deviation (SD) $= \sqrt{\Sigma (A_i - E(A))^2 B_i} = 2179$

A number of such costs, of varying degrees of uncertainty, may make up a total (revenues may also be included as negative costs).

The expected value of the total is always the sum of the expected value of the individual costs. Thus, an expected profit figure may be calculated by aggregating all the individual expected costs and revenues. For most organisations, this result hopefully confirms current practice! This point will be resumed later.

What of the standard deviation of the total? This is most emphatically not the total of the individual standard deviations *unless* there is an expected perfect positive correlation (+1) between the classifications[26]. This is a very unlikely prospect as regards costs; it is even more unlikely if revenues are also included, for perfect positive correlation would imply that when costs are below their expected value, revenues are above theirs – what we would commonly understand as an inverse relationship.

Normally there will be a 'diversifying effect', correlation is less than +1 and costs and revenues will move, in varying degrees, independently of each other. Thus, when one cost is greatly above average another cost may be just above average, creating an offsetting effect. The standard deviation of the total is therefore somewhat less than the sum of the parts. The precise formula is:

$$\text{SD(Total)} = \sqrt{\underset{i \ j}{\Sigma\Sigma}\text{Covariance Class}_i \text{ Class}_j}$$

where class = classification, and the subscripts i and j are used to identify the various classifications. In words, this is the square root of the sum of all possible covariances[27]. Note that where i = j the covariance is the variance of that particular classification.

The practical estimation of the standard deviation is beyond the scope of this monograph. However, an example often quoted to illustrate the aggregation effect concerns the summation of costs that are independent of each other and therefore have zero covariance with other costs. In this special case the formula is:

$$SD(Total) = \sqrt{\sum_i Variance\ (Class_i)}$$

Thus, if a total repair budget was for ten machines and the estimate for each machine was as in the example above. Then, assuming zero covariance or correlation between repair bills the aggregate figures are:

$$E\ (Total\ repairs) = 10 \times 10500 = £105000$$

$$SD\ (Total) = \sqrt{10 \times 2179^2} = £6891$$

Only if the repair bills were perfectly correlated would the standard deviation of the total be £21 790.

Although the standard deviation of £6891 is higher than the individual £2179 deviations, relative to the expected value it is less. This figure is known as the coefficient of variation:

$$coefficient\ of\ variation\ (CV) = \frac{standard\ deviation}{expected\ value}$$

$$CV\ (repair\ bill\ machine\ 1) = \frac{2179}{10500} \times 100 = 20.8\%$$

$$CV\ (total\ repair\ budget) = \frac{6991}{105000} \times 100 = 6.6\%$$

In that uncertainty in estimation is unwelcome, the reduction in the coefficient of variation is beneficial. There is, though, a special case where this effect may deceive. Take the example quoted above, suppose that instead of declaring the expected value as the budget repair cost for each machine, a tougher budget was set at, say a ½ standard deviation below the mean at 10,500 – (½) 2179 = £9410.5. If the probability distribution is taken as an approximation of a normal distribution then there is about a 30 per cent chance of meeting this budget for an individual machine. But the chance of meeting the overall budget is considerably less than 30 per cent. Taking the overall distribution of probable returns to be also approximately normal, there is only a 6 per cent chance that the total will be 9410.5 × 10 = £94105, the total of the tough budgets![28]

Alternatively, if the budget is set at ½ standard deviation above the mean at: 10500 + (½) 2179 = £11589.5 for each machine (there will be about a 70 per cent chance of achieving the budget for each machine), then there will be a 94 per cent chance of achieving the total of 11589.5 × 10 = £115895.[29]

If the total is the sum of the expected value of the costs this disparity between the probability of achieving the individual budget and the total budget is avoided. Where this is not the case the greater the degree of positive correlation between the costs the less the disparity.[30]

In conclusion, the uncertainty of an aggregate of estimates may be very different from the uncertainty of the estimates themselves. Of particular importance, as has been shown, is the degree of correlation or covariance between individual classifications.

3.4 The accounting contribution

The accounting profession has, over the years, developed several commonly accepted techniques for classifying and presenting accounting data. The following two sections summarise the important elements of the accounting contribution that have not been described elsewhere.

3.4.1 The presentation of classifications

Most accounting classifications when used for management purposes appear in the form of an accounting report. The presentation of such reports can be summarised by the following four rules:

(1) Totals are divided on the basis of time and one further attribute.

(2) The order of presentation is from the general to the particular. The first pages of a report contain highly aggregared data, succeeding pages divide the figures into increasing detail.

(3) Information is presented on a periodic basis.

(4) The same report format and classes of data are maintained over time.

Taking the report in Table 3.5 as an example, rule 1 is obeyed in that total controllable costs are divided according to the attribute 'subject of expense' (see Section 3.4.2). Furthermore, division is a complete subdivision of the total cost; this is ensured by the inclusion of the catch-all classification 'Other costs' (see Section 1.2.1). Rule 2 is obeyed by the presentation of the larger classification first[31]. Rules 3 and 4 simply require the same format to be presented on a regular basis.

Commonly accepted exceptions to these rules are:

(1) The reporting structure should be sufficiently flexible to be able to produce special reports from time to time.
(2) Reports may analyse totals using two attributes (other than time) in matrix format.

For example, the labour report in Table 3.6 illustrates the use of the attributes 'administrative division' and 'subject' expense type to analyse the total cost of £745,000. The matrix format also includes the classification 'administrative division' *and* expense type.

Table 3.6 The classification of labour costs on the basis of more than one attribute (£000s)

	Production	Marketing	HQ	Total
Direct labour	280	20	—	300
Indirect labour	50	100	—	150
Administration	20	20	15	55
Management services	20	20	200	240
	370	160	215	745

Thus the £745,000 total labour cost may be classified by division alone, i.e. Production £370,000, Marketing £160,000 and HQ £215,000, or by subject alone, i.e., Direct labour £300,000, Indirect labour £130,000, Administration £55,000 and Management Services £240,000, or finally by both attributes, e.g., Direct labour in Production division £280,000, Indirect labour in Production division £50,000 and so on. Although these reports provide considerably more information than the traditional format, this is only achieved at the expense of greater processing costs.

3.4.2 Traditional classifications

Almost all classifications in accounting systems use at least one of the following attributes[32].

(1) Time when incurred, e.g., day, month or year.
(2) Behaviour in relation to production, e.g., direct or indirect costs, variable, semi-variable and fixed costs.
(3) Subjective form. This attribute divides data according to the type of attribute involved. For example, in Table 3.5 total controllable costs are divided according to subject, i.e. types of labour, materials and overheads.
(4) Objective form. In this case data is divided according to its object or purpose; examples include the cost of product A or revenue from product B.
(5) Costing systems such as job costing, process costing, contract costing, marginal costing and standard costing, lead to certain unique classifications of data. For example, a labour variance and an equivalent unit are classifications special to standard costing and process costing systems, respectively.
(6) Control. Costs may be seen as controllable or uncontrollable, avoidable or unavoidable. In the same manner, revenues may be seen as attributable, and therefore to some extent controllable, or non-attributable to a particular entity.
(7) Responsibility. This attribute usually refers to the same costs and revenues as the previous attribute; thus the responsibility for transactions is assigned to the manager or department who has control over them.
(8) Decisions. Several classifications are derived from the study of decisions within the organisation. The more generally accepted terms are relevant cost, differential cost, opportunity cost and marginal cost.
(9) Special subject reports that examine value added, cash flow, productivity and other subjects will produce special classifications, such as value added per employee, cash flow from debtors, and so on.

A classification will make use of one or more of these attributes, for instance, 'Department C labour costs for period 8' uses attributes 1, 3 and 7, or 'Standard material cost for product B' uses attributes 3, 4 and 5. The attribute values will depend upon the particular circumstances of the company and will determine, for instance, the particular materials and types of labour used for attribute 3, the type of costing system for 5, and so on.

An important subset of classifications are those required for external reporting. These classifications have, over the years, become increasingly standardised by the requirements of the Stock Exchange Rules and Regulations (for quoted companies), the Companies Act 1981 Schedule 1, Statements of Standard Accounting Practice and now the Fourth Directive of the EEC. The reader is referred to these sources for further details. Attempts have been made to extend this uniformity to internal reporting requirements, for example, the management accounting sections of the French Plan Comptable. This and other attempts have failed, except in cases where the information is required for external reports where there is a need for comparative data[33]. The prevailing dictum for internal purposes would seem to be 'my firm is different'[34].

In general, standardisation should not be seen as solving the question as to how a firm should classify its accounts. It merely details the requirements of one particular set of users, which, in the case of the Annual Report or its equivalent, are those external to the organisation. Whether such classifications meet the requirements of internal management or more generally the intended beneficiaries is still subject to the issues and problems outlined in this study. In addition, the methodologies as discussed in Chapter 2 are no less applicable to the decisions of external users merely because there are certain legal requirements for the disclosure of data.

3.4.3 *Evaluation of the traditional accounting approach*

The main strength of the traditional accounting concepts as described in the previous two sections is that it offers several well understood classifications in a helpful format. Textbooks contain ample analysis of their use in planning, decision making and control as well as giving extensive definitions. Typical examples include: the use of fixed and variable costs for cost – volume – profit analysis; the inclusion or otherwise of overhead costs in product costing and the definition of relevant costs, standard costs and process costs. Furthermore the traditional presentation of the data (Section 3.4.1) offers a clear picture as to how overall costs are analysed. As a result, the effects of a change of cost in a detailed classification may be traced through to more aggregated data, and the derivation of complex classifications such as production cost and profit, are clearly explained.

The weaknesses stem from the fact that the accounting approach was devised at a time when non-computerised systems predominated. The limited information-processing resources severely restricted the number of classifications that could be chosen. As a result the emphasis of the approach is on deriving a single best set of classifications to suit all purposes. Inevitably there is not a particularly 'good fit' between some of the uses of the data and the chosen set of classifications, especially for those uses that are beyond the immediate scope of the accountant. It is only in the last decade, with the introduction of more powerful database systems that the concept put forward in this study of different classifications for different goals has begun to provide an improved basis for the design of accounting information systems. *Kaplan*[35] expresses this development as follows:

As accountants sought cost accounting procedures that would be relevant for many different planning decisions and control actions, they realised that cost aggregations or allocations should vary as a function of the decision being made with the cost data. No unique cost assignment was relevant for all decisions. This was the start of management accounting which emphasises cost allocations for internal decisions and control rather than for financial reporting. Horngren refers to this user orientated or decision model approach to cost accounting as the conditional truth approach; that is, truth depends on how the cost assignment will be used.

3.5 Summary and conclusions

This chapter has examined the issues involved in converting classifications into account and reports. These may be summarised briefly as:

(1) *The problem of selection.* Recording the attributes of accounting transactions can result in many potential classifications. In order to avoid over capacity, there is, therefore, a need to limit data requirements. The main method for achieving this end is to use the decision models developed in the previous chapter. The relevance of the variables may also be tested by use of the law of requisite variety (see Section 3.2).

(2) *Aggregation.* Most classifications are derived from summing or aggregating individual transactions. This results in an inevitable loss of information as the details of each transaction are concealed within the total figure. In Section 3.3 a measure of aggregation was developed that could be used as a critique of the aggregation level in an accounting report. Where the aggregation is of estimates, it was shown in Section 3.3.3 that aggregate uncertainty depended upon the covariance of the individual classifications.

(3) *The accounting contribution.* The study of accounting and accounting practice has over the years developed several guidelines for presenting data as well as some useful bases for classification. This contribution was summarised and assessed in Section 3.4.

4
Coding

4.1 *Introduction*

A code was described in Chapter 1 as being a collection of symbols used to carry information within the organisation. That information is determined by the way in which data is classified. A code for a materials account, for instance, requires a classification of materials in order to define the attributes to be coded. Coding may therefore be regarded as the consequence of classification.

This chapter provides a guide to designing a code. The first section describes the qualities of a good code. The succeeding two sections examine the main issues involved in selecting a code, namely, the type of code (Section 4.3), and the means of avoiding coding errors (Section 4.4). In the final section the effects of computer developments are described and assessed.

4.2 *Qualities of good coding*

A good code is one that serves the needs of the organisation. The first step, therefore, in designing a code is to determine what those needs are. This may be done by considering each of the qualities listed below and then ranking them in order of importance. The exercise should serve as a basis for subsequent design.

4.2.1 *Uniqueness*

Each value of a code should have a unique meaning. For example, an invoice number should identify or be associated with one particular invoice; a part number should refer to one particular part, a sales area code should identify one particular area and so on. A code or portion of a code that identifies uniquely the item being encoded is called a key. An invoice number, for instance, is a key, in that only one invoice can have that number, whereas a sales area code is not a key with respect to the invoice, in that many invoices may have the same area code. This aspect of uniqueness is important in the subsequent computerisation of the system.

4.2.2 Expandability

There should be room for development in a code. The nine digit code in Table 4.1, for example, is limited in two ways.

Firstly, in its present format it is not possible to add another attribute, such as sales area, to the code. Such an extension could only be incorporated by the costly alternative of opening up another file and creating a separate code relating area to the key element of the code, which is the invoice number. If there were spare numbers in the code, developments could be incorporated with far less disruption to the existing system.

A second way in which the code is limited is in the number of values that each attribute may have. In Table 4.1, only ten product categories, 100 customer numbers and 10,000 invoice numbers can be included. Most firms' needs would exceed such a limited capacity.

Table 4.1 A fixed-length sales code

Digit	1234	56	7	89
Attribute	Invoice No.	Customer No.	Product category	Month

4.2.3 Errors

A code, and the administration associated with it, should be designed in such a way as to reduce coding errors to an acceptable level (see section 4.4).

4.2.4 Significance

Where staff are involved directly in using codes, it is helpful if the codes convey the required information in an orderly manner. For instance, it would be easier for staff to remember and check an account code in say department X, if all such codes began with a particular number, rather than an arbitrarily assigned number.

4.2.5 Mnemonics

The benefits of significance are further enhanced by the use of mnemonic devices that help the user to relate a code to its meaning. As an example, an account concerning labour may begin with the letter 'L' or an account for materials may begin with 'M'. Also, there may be gaps or marks such as ' Y ' or '–' dividing up the elements of the code, thus making it easier to memorise.

4.2.6 Format

A well designed code should maintain the same format or structure for clarity and ease of management. This quality is, in any case, a normal requirement of the information system. It is the need to maintain the same format that is the source of many of the problems of expandibility.

4.2.7 Conciseness

In many cases the desirable qualities of a code set out above can be gained only at the expense of greater length. Counterbalancing these qualities are the handling and processing advantages of brevity.

4.2.8 Sortability

All systems require the user to indicate how codes are to be sorted. This is often reflected in the design of the code itself; a common example is the need to sort sales invoices into alphabetical order by customer. It would be helpful in such cases if the customer number reflected alphabetical order. Thus customer code 00 could be used for A Ltd and 01 for B Ltd, and so on. Unfortunately, an expandibility problem is created, if in this example the company sells to AB Ltd, a suitable code cannot be allocated. It may therefore be necessary to leave gaps in the code. This problem is examined further in the next section.

4.3 Types of code

The design of a code is made up of three basic aspects; (1) *The length*. (2) *The symbols*. (3) *The significance*. The range of possibilities for each aspect is illustrated in Figure 4.1.

Figure 4.1 Aspects of code design

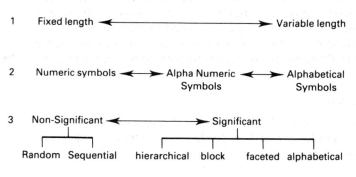

1 Fixed length ←————————————→ Variable length

2 Numeric symbols ←——→ Alpha Numeric ←——→ Alphabetical
                          Symbols   Symbols

3 Non-Significant ←————————→ Significant

   Random Sequential   hierarchical   block   faceted alphabetical

The code in Table 4.1 for instance is a fixed length, numerical, faceted code, whereas local telephone numbers are variable length, numeric and random codes. This section examines each of these qualities and their value in code design.

4.3.1 Length

- *Fixed.* Most modern systems require the user to limit the number of characters assigned to a code.

- *Variable.* Space may be saved by using a varying number of symbols, with shorter codes reserved for the more commonly used subjects. The old STD telephone code is an example of this, London being 01, Manchester 061 and Leicester 0533. Variable length is ideally suited to progressive codes, where categories are subdivided into greater detail[36]. Variable-length codes may always be converted into fixed codes by adding zeros; the three STD codes, for instance, could be converted into a 4-digit fixed-length code with London and Manchester being 0100 and 0610, respectively[37].

4.3.2 Symbols

- *Numeric.* Most codes in accounting are numeric. This is despite the fact that an equivalent code using letters would be shorter. The advantage of using numeric symbols is that it is easier to determine the order and structure of information within the code, e.g., 0 to 100 is easier to appreciate than, say, the similar range A0 to J9. This quality benefits both user and programmer.

- *Non-numeric.* A code may be alphabetical or alpha numeric (letters and numbers) and it may also contain symbols such as '&' or '*'. An alphabetical code will have 26 alternatives per character, an alpha numeric code 36 alternatives and a numeric code only 10. Thus a three-character code will have $26^3 = 17,576$ combinations if it is alphabetical, $36^3 = 46,656$ if it is alpha numeric and only $10^3 = 1,000$ combinations if it is a numeric code. Other symbols may be necessary for segmenting or dividing up a code where the segments are of variable length, i.e., the divisions will occur at varying points in the code; such divisions are not needed for fixed-length segments, but may nevertheless improve presentation.

4.3.3 Significance

- *Non-significant codes.* These codes are confined to identifying or acting as a key for an item being coded, as such they provide a tag or label to which other more significant information may be attached.

The code may be random or sequential. A random code requires the user to look up the next available number; this can be used as a means of avoiding accidental duplication where several people are required to enter the codes. A similar effect, however, can be achieved by using a sequential code with a special stamp.

- *Significant codes.* This is a category that contains many codes whose distinguishing feature is that they convey information about the item being encoded. In most cases the code will also be required to provide a unique identification.

These two requirements usually result in a longer code than the non-significant equivalent. For instance, one significant account code encountered during background research used 12 digits, giving a capacity that vastly exceeded the 170 accounts actually needed.

The following are the main types of significant code.

Block codes

This is a grouping of items according to a particular attribute. As an example, *Bigg's Cost Accounts*[38] recommends grouping accounts according to the type of expenditure involved:

Assets	0000 – 1999
Liabilities	2000 – 2999
Cost centres	3000 – 3999
Income	4000 – 4999
Expenditure	5000 – 6999
Miscellaneous	7000 – 9999

Such a code may be progressive, i.e., there are further smaller divisions within each block. For instance, the section devoted to assets can be further subdivided into raw material stocks 1000–1149, component stocks 1150–1299, consumable stocks 1300–1500, and so on.

A blocked code has the qualities of significance, mnemonics and sortability outlined in Section 4.2. Using the example above, significance is enhanced by the fact that, for example, all numbers below 3000 are balance sheet items. If a B was used as a prefix to such codes, then they would also be mnemonic. Sortability is obviously enhanced by grouping the observations according to the likely basis of retrieval.

The disadvantages of a blocked code are that it can only contain information about a single attribute; thus the code in this example is confined to the subject of the account; also, because the limits of each block have to be determined when the code is first designed, there is inevitably an expandibility problem.

Alphabetical code

When coding names such as customers, suppliers and employers, it is often the case that the system requires the order of the code to match the alphabetical order. An alphabetical code converts names into a numerical code that attempts to preserve alphabetical order by allowing more space for more common names. One such code is known as SOUNDEX. This method takes the first letter of the name as the first character of the code followed by three digits representing the next three letters, excluding W, H and Y and the vowels. The conversion of letters into numbers is according to the table below:

Use 1 for B, F, P, V
    2 for C, G, J, K, Q, S, X, Z
    3 for D, T
    4 for L
    5 for M, N
    6 for R

Thus Jones B would be J521 and Smith R would be S536. This method does not guarantee that each name is assigned a unique code, and therefore some modification might be needed.

Hierarchical code

This code arranges items according to an established order such as weight, length, diameter, size, organisational ranks, etc., and is useful if such hierarchies are important in the subsequent analysis of the data.

Faceted or chain code

This form of code is by far the most common in present day computerised information systems. The code consists of a series of attributes deemed relevant for the item being encoded. Each attribute is described by a section within the code known as a field. Within each field, information is kept in blocked sequential or random order. Figure 4.2 gives an example of an account code of a firm that took part in the background research. Information within each field was blocked; thus all administrative salaries had a final field beginning fourteen no matter the company, division or department, etc. The drawback of storing so much information within one code is the length required. In this particular example, less than 0.00027 per cent of the possible space was used.

Figure 4.2 A faceted or chain code

Code	3	4	1	0	0	0	0	8	1	4	0	0

Fields

Company

Division

Department

Not used

Revenue, expense or balance sheet item

Account subject

Classification code

This form of code is similar to the faceted code, except that there is a progressive relationship between the fields; each subsequent field represents a further subdivision of the previous one. The most famous example of such a code is the Dewey Decimal System used for classifying books in libraries. The example below illustrates the way in which the categories develop; level and balance, in this instance, is concerned with the mechanical aspect of machines which is classified as a branch of physics which is in turn a natural science:

500	Natural Sciences
510	Mathematics
520	Astronomy
530	Physics
531	Mechanics
531.1	Machines
531.11	Level and Balance

The qualities of this code are similar to those of the faceted, blocked and variable-length codes, of which it is a particular extension.

4.4 Coding errors

A typical medium-sized firm will code thousands of financial transactions per month. It is inevitable that even in the most sophisticated of systems a certain number of coding errors will occur. Such errors are liable to result in the presentation of misleading data and thereby defeat the whole purpose of the accounting system. It is therefore important that the organisation develops a clear policy for detecting and preventing errors.

4.4.1 Types of error

The following list represents the main types of error that can occur:

- *Misinterpretation.* Here, a valid code is mistakenly entered owing to a misreading of the coding manual or a misinterpretation of the item to be encoded.
- *Transposition error.* This occurs when the symbols of a code, usually adjacent, are given in reverse order e.g. 1234 input as 1324.
- *Transcription error.* In this case a symbol in a code is mistakenly replaced by another, e.g., 1234 input as 1284.
- *Random error.* This error is a combination of the previous two errors, and includes the accidental addition or omission of symbols.
- *System-based error.* Poor programming and faulty hardware can cause items to be miscoded within the system.

4.4.2 Error detection

Most errors occur when data is being coded; that is, when the code is selected and entered into the system. It is no coincidence that this is also the point where human intervention is at its greatest.

The following five factors summarise the main issues in error detection.

(1) Documentation

All information systems require documents as the original source of data. Typical examples include expense forms, invoices, costing sheets and so on. Many systems also require codes to be listed manually before being entered in batches into the computer system. In all cases, the firm should take great care that the forms bearing codes are clearly designed and properly completed. Conventions must be agreed that distinguish between the letters and numbers I and 1, Z and 2, O and 0. Different coloured forms may be used to emphasise their differing purposes. Headings and instructions should be clearly laid out and simple checks, such as ensuring that all documents have been submitted and that double-entry transactions balance, should be carried out. Document-related errors that do occur should be carefully analysed and adjustments to the relevant forms made where necessary.

(2) *Environment*

The conditions of work for coding clerks can have an important influence on the quality of their work. Their task is not easy. Total accuracy is required for a job that is both repetitive and dull.

In order to help them in this task, attention should be paid to the design of the office, the quality of seating, the level of lighting and brightness of the video screen. Employers should be mindful of evidence that poor conditions for coding data can damage employees' health[37]. Job rotation at the clerical level should be encouraged as a means of providing variety and important back-up facilities in case of illness.

(3) *Code length*

Some firms seem to take an almost perverse pleasure in using long codes. It is as if length is taken as an indication of the system's sophistication. A systems analyst interviewed in the background research found that one organisation used a 30-digit code, while 12-digit codes such as that in Figure 4.2 are not uncommon. In fact a long code is usually an indication of a poorly designed system. Unnecessary length occurs where the user is being asked to record attributes that could more efficiently be stored elsewhere. For example, the code in Figure 4.2 could omit the 'Division' and 'Company' and 'Department' attributes from the account code and store the information separately in a code relating these attributes to a Key Field which is also stored as part of the account number.

Where there is human involvement in the coding of data, the longer the code, the greater the probability of error. Researchers have conducted tests to try and establish how long a code can be before there is a significant increase in the error rate. The most widely accepted result is from the work of *Miller*[40], who found that the human short-term memory can reliably retain seven digits plus or minus two. Other work has suggested that errors are reduced when codes can easily be split up or partitioned e.g. six-figure telephone numbers read as 23-45-67. The use of alpha numeric codes can help such partitioning[41].

(4) *Code design – check digits*

Where there is human involvement in handling codes there will, even with the most carefully designed of codes, always be errors in coding. It may be easier to detect the error after it has occurred rather than trying to prevent it occurring. Such detection can be built into the design of a code itself, by means of a check digit. Where this approach is used the last symbol of the code is a mathematical function of the previous symbols; this function and hence the code itself is checked by the computer whenever a code is entered, and if an error is detected, the clerk cannot enter any more data until he has corrected it.

A simple example of a check digit is where the third digit of a three-figure code is calculated as the remainder from dividing the first two digits by 7. Thus the code 361 would be valid, because $36 \div 7 = 5$ with a remainder 1, which is indeed the last digit of the code. If the code were misread as 341 (a transcription error), the computer would reject the entry, because $34 \div 7 = 4$ with a remainder of 6 and not 1. Similarly if two figures were transposed and the code was input as say 631 then it would be rejected, because $63 \div 7 = 9$ with a remainder 0 and not 1. Unfortunately, not all errors would be detected by this particular method. If, for instance, the code 184 were input as 814, the error would not be detected because both 18 and 81 when divided by 7 have a remainder of 4.

In order to minimise the acceptance within a system of incorrect codes which pass the check digit test, mathematicians have devised special algorithms. The most commonly accepted method is as follows:

- Step 1   Each digit of a code is multiplied by a predetermined weight.
- Step 2   The result of Step 1 is then totalled and divided by a figure called the modulus.
- Step 3   The check digit is calculated as the remainder when the result of Step 2 is subtracted from the modulus.

If a modulus of 13 or more is chosen in Step 2, then any weights are acceptable. If the modulus is below this amount, then weights of 'oscillating arithmetic progression' should be used. These weights ascend from 1 to a value of just below half the modulus and then descend from the modulus minus 1 to just above half the modulus.

For example, a six-digit code 316858 using modulus 11 would have the weights 1,2,3,4,5,10. The check digit for such a code is calculated as shown in Table 4.2.

Table 4.2 Calculating check digits

Step 1	Multiply the digits by predetermined weights				
	Code	×	Weight	=	Total
	3	×	1	=	3
	1	×	2	=	2
	6	×	3	=	18
	8	×	4	=	32
	5	×	5	=	25
	8	×	10	=	80
					160
Step 2	Divide the total by the modulus				
	$160 \div 11 = 14$ remainder 6				
Step 3	Subtract the remainder from the modulus $11 - 6 = 5$				
	Full code is therefore 3168585.				

Usually only one character is allowed as the check digit. Where the formula requires more than one digit, it is normal to use a letter or symbol instead. Where the modulus is 11 or over, 100 per cent of transcription and transposition errors are detected. The percentage of random errors detected is calculated by the formula $(1-1/m) \times 100$ where m is the modulus. Thus Modulus 11 detects $(1-1/11) \times 100 = 90.9$ per cent of random errors.

Alphanumeric codes obey the same rules as numeric codes. The letters are treated as a continuation of the numerical sequence; hence $A=10, B=11 \ldots Z=35$. Modulus 37 detects all transcription and transposition errors in alphanumeric codes and 97.3 per cent of random errors (i.e., $[1-1/37] \times 100$).

Other means

Finally, errors may be detected without direct reference to code design or the coding process. A review of postings to accounts may reveal unusually large or small amounts charged to certain accounts; other accounts may atypically have no entries against them, or a series of small entries where only one is expected.

In management accounts, where actual and budget figures are compared, unexpected variances may indicate miscoded items. In addition, statement reconciliations, bank reconciliations, stock takes and general analysis of financial data may all reveal miscoded transactions. Although the organisation should make every effort to avoid correcting errors at this late stage in the processing of data, the existence of coding errors can never be ruled out.

4.5 *Computer developments and coding*

Developments in computer hardware are tending to reduce human intervention by automating the transfer of data between source documents and the computer. One such system uses light pens that automatically convert the bars into code numbers when they are traced across printed bar codes. Many libraries in the United Kingdom use this technique to record the movement of library books.

Code numbers may be directly read by the computer using a Magnetic Ink Character Recognition System (MICR) or the Optical Mark Character Recognition System (OMCR). The MICR system prints codes using ferrous oxide ink, which is magnetised just before being read by the computer. This system is used for cheques. The OMCR system uses photoelectric cells to detect the presence or otherwise of pencil marks on particular areas of source documents. The computer will automatically code data from these simple observations. Finally, voice-recognition systems[42] promise to make it easier for humans to communicate data to the computer, though at present such systems are in their early stages.

The increased use of computer hardware has had the effect of reducing coding costs, increasing the capacity of the system and making the coding process quicker and more reliable. In the future it is not unreasonable to expect that the physical process of coding and storing data will present virtually no problems for an information system.

There have also been significant advances in the programming of computers that have made possible the following developments with respect to coding:

(1) Codes may be better structured to suit the user. This can be done by
(a) concealing unused portions of the code from the user;
(b) automatically entering certain parts of the code where it is common to a particular user or terminal and (c) structuring the information in the code to reduce its length.
(2) The use of codes may be made more flexible. Traditional code design tends to favour the retrieval of information in a certain manner. Modern computer systems are designed to encode data in such a way as to increase the flexibility of use or data independence.
(3) Code conversion tables may be used. Firms are often reluctant to adopt new codes where staff are familiar with existing ones. The introduction of a new system often means a change of code, where

there is a one-to-one correspondence between the old and new codes; this translation can be done within the system. User-friendly codes may also be converted to more efficient forms for computer handling without disturbing the user.

(4) Coding manuals may be computerised. Interactive programs may be used to help the user find the correct code.

These and other advances are contributing to making the coding process a less obtrusive part of the system. This imposes a new responsibility on the accountant, for now that the coding and decoding of data is less difficult, the accountant must specify the way in which these developments can be exploited; hence the importance of the classification methodology of Chapter 2.

4.6 Summary and conclusions

In the past, codes – especially account codes – were seen as the responsibility of the accountant. The development of computerised information systems has now transferred much of this responsibility to the computer specialist. The accountant need now concern himself less with the detailed design of the code and more with ensuring that his requirements are fulfilled by the system. To this end, this chapter has reviewed the coding decision by examining the desirable qualities of a code (Section 4.2), the forms of code in common use (Section 4.3) and the problem of coding errors (Section 4.4). Further developments in computing (Section 4.5) promise to reduce rather than increase the accountant's direct involvement with this aspect of the information system.

5
Conclusions

Classification and coding of financial data are essential activities in an accounting information system. Despite their importance, many traditional textbooks have given the subject somewhat cursory treatment. It is only recently, due to the development of information technology, that the full implications of the subject have been explored. This study is based upon these advances and upon the recent developments in management accounting, summarised as follows:

(1) Decisions, planning and control within an organisation, depend upon appropriate classifications of information. Consequently, an analysis of classifications should be based upon the decisions and the organisation structure to which they relate.

(2) The greater data processing ability of the computer has meant that the user need no longer resort to a standard set of classifications, but should actively seek to adapt a system that suits his own requirements. Only by doing this will the user fully exploit the capabilities of the computer.

(3) The advances in information technology have been accompanied by new concepts and new terminology in the classification and coding of data. These advances should be incorporated into the accounting system.

(4) The problems of system design and data management associated with classification and coding have increasingly become specialised tasks. The accountant must seek to develop the accounting system as a member of a data management team. Issues in designing reports and accounts cannot therefore be regarded as relating solely to the accounting function.

The relationship that classification and coding has with decision-making indicates the need for an organisation regularly to review its treatment of data. The aim of this study has been to aid such reviews by describing the processes of classification and coding as well as analysing the problems and issues involved.

References

1 For examples *see* Wald, J., *Bigg's Cost Accounts*, 10th Edn, Macdonald and Evans, 1978, p.321, or Matz, A., and Usry, M.F., *Cost Accounting Planning and Control*, 6th Edn, South Western Publishing, 1976, p.63.

2 *As in the French* 'Plan Comptable', see Nobes, C.W., and Parker, R.H., *Comparative International Accounting*, Philip Allen, 1981, p.66, or *The Companies Act 1981 Sch 1*, HMSO.

3 A similar definition is given in: Lee, B., *Introducing Systems Analysis and Design*, Vol. 2, NCC Publications, 1979, p.384, and an abbreviated version in: *Management Accounting: Official Terminology of the ICMA*, 1974. p.5.

4 *See* Chapter 2 for further analysis.

5 Klimoski, *et al.* 'Human information processing', In Livingstone, J.L. (Ed) *Managerial Accounting: The Behavioral Foundations*, Grid 1975 p.177.

6 Edwardes, M. *Back from the Brink*, Collins, 1983, p.52.

7 *Management Accounting: Official Terminology of the ICMA*, 1974, p.47.

8 For instance *See* Martin J. *'Principles of Data-Base Management'* Prentice Hall 1976.

9 Johnson, T.H., Kaplan, R.S., *'Relevance Lost: The rise and fall of management accounting'* Harvard Business School Press, 1987, p.1.

10 Kaplan, R.S., Atkinson, A.A., *'Advanced Management Accounting'* Second Edition 1989 p.372 et seq.

11 Kaplan, R.S., Atkinson, A.A., op cit p.191 et seq.

12 Wilson, R.M.S., 'Strategic Cost Analysis' 'Management Accounting' October 1990 and Bromwich, M., Bhimani, A. 'Strategic Investment Appraisal' London Business School Discussion Paper in Accounting and Finance No. 89/1.

13 *See* Date, C.J., *An Introduction to Database Systems*, 3rd Edn, Addison-Wesley, 1981, pp.10–13.

14 Martin, J., *Strategic Data Planning Methodologies*, Prentice Hall, 1982, p.143.

15 For a more computer-orientated approach, *see* Martin, J., *op. cit.*, p.99.

16 Martin, J., *op. cit.*, p.132.

17 *See* Arnold, J., *Pricing and Output Decision*, Haymarket, 1973, p.13; Carsberg, B., *Economics of Business Decisions*, Penguin, 1975, p.35; Bromwich, M., The Economics of Capital Budgeting, Penguin, 1976, p.20; Sizer, J., *An Insight into Management Accounting*, Penguin, 1979, p.22.

18 Carsberg, B., *'The Economics of Business Decisions'*, Penguin 1975, p.35.

19 Cyert, R., and March, J.G., *A Behavioral Theory of the Firm*, Prentice Hall, 1963, p.28.

20 In addition to the references in note 12, *see* Daniels, A., and Yeates, D., *Practical Systems Design*, Pitman, 1984, p.76.

21 For example, *see* Koutsoyiannis, A., *Modern Microeconomics*, Macmillan, 1979, p.62.

22 *See* Davis, G.B., *Management Information Systems Concept and Foundations Structure and Development*, McGraw-Hill, 1974, p.97.

23 Base 2 for the logarithm is chosen to conform to other concepts in information theory; any base may be used for this purpose.

24 Horngren, C.T., *Cost Accounting: A Managerial Emphasis*, 4th Edn, Prentice-Hall, 1985, p.189. For further reading on this concept see Mace, R., *Managerial Information and the Computer*, Haymarket, 1974, p.41 *et seq.*

25 Fox, R., Kennedy, A., Sugden, K., *'Decision Making: A management accounting perspective'* Butterworth-Heinemann 1990, p.56.

26 For the more mathematically minded, proof of the proposition that where there is an expected perfect positive correlation between classifications, the standard deviation of the total is the sum of the individual standard deviations as follows:

Let $X_i = \Sigma_j X_i^{\,j}$ where superscript j represents a classification and i an observation and the correlation $(X^i, X^j) = 1$ for all i and j.

Then $SD(X^i) \times SD(X^j) = Cov(X^i, X^j)$.

Using the formula in the text:

$$SD(X_i) = \sqrt{\underset{i\ j}{\Sigma\Sigma} SD(X^i)SD(X^j)}$$

$$= \sqrt{(\underset{i}{\Sigma} SD(X^i))^2}$$

$$= \underset{i}{\Sigma} SD(X^i)$$

which is the summation of the standard deviation of each classification QED.

27 Remembering that the covariance is a non-standardised correlation, where the correlation between two populations X_i and Y_i is:

$$\frac{\text{covariance (XY)}}{SD\,(X)\,SD\,(Y)}$$

and covariance is

$$\Sigma[X_i - E(X)][Y_i - E(Y)] \, pr\,(X_i, Y_i)$$

where pr (X_i, Y_i) is the probability of X_i and Y_i occurring together.

28 The standard deviation of the total is 6891 (see text), the total of the tough budgets is therefore:

$$\frac{105000 - 94105}{6891} = 1.58$$

standard deviations below the mean. Assuming the overall distribution to be approximately normal, there is a 6 per cent chance of achieving this figure or less using a standard normal probability density curve.

29 As the normal distribution is symmetric this is merely the other tail of the normal curve i.e. 1.58 standard deviations above the mean.

30 From note 28, it is clear that the higher the standard deviation of the budget total the lower the standardised distance of the total from the total mean – the less the disparity. The higher the correlation between classifications the greater the standard deviation of the total, thus achieving this effect.

31 It is not always the case that information is presented in size order; conventions and the need for consistency of format over time may dictate otherwise.

32 A similar list may be found in Horngren, C.T., *op.cit.*, p.34 (more recent editions co-authored by Foster, G.) and Drury, C., *Management and Cost Accounting*, Chapman Hall 1988.

33 As is the case in certain Eastern European countries.

34 *See* Richard, J., 'A history of international accounting practices', *Issues in Accountability*, No.10, pp.7–26.

35 Kaplan, R.S., *Advanced Management Accounting*, Prentice Hall, 1st Edition 1982, p.2.

36 *See* Section 4.3.3.

37 This would require a complete revision of the telephone number format.

38 Wald, J., *Bigg's Cost Accounts*, 10th Edn, Macdonald & Evans, 1978, p.321.

39 *See New Scientist*, 23 May 1985, p.7.

40 Miller, G.A., 'The magical number seven plus or minus two: some limitations on our capability for processing information', *The Psychological Review*, March 1956, pp.81–97.

41 *See* Davis, G.B., *op.cit.*, p.69.

42 *New Scientist*, 1 November 1984, p.22.